Brandon Ingram: The Inspiring Story of One of Basketball's Star Forwards

An Unauthorized Biography

By: Clayton Geoffreys

Table of Contents

Foreword

When he first entered the league, it was widely believed that Brandon Ingram would play many years alongside Lonzo Ball as the next generation of the Los Angeles Lakers. That original vision quickly changed upon the decision by LeBron James to sign with the Lakers in the summer of 2018. Before long, the young core of Ball and Ingram were traded to the New Orleans Pelicans in a blockbuster deal for All-Star Anthony Davis as the Lakers pivoted to win-now mode. This trade ultimately turned out to be a blessing for Ingram; in just his first season with the Pelicans, he made his first All-Star selection and was named the Most Improved Player of the league. It'll be exciting to see what New Orleans can put together as Ingram plays alongside Zion Williamson and other talented young players. Thank you for purchasing *Brandon Ingram: The Inspiring Story of One of Basketball's Star Forwards*. In this unauthorized biography, we will learn Brandon Ingram's incredible life story and impact on the game of basketball. Hope you enjoy and if you do, please do not forget to leave a review!

Also, check out my website at claytongeoffreys.com to join my exclusive list where I let you know about my latest books. To thank you for your purchase, you can go to my site to download a free copy of *33 Life Lessons: Success Principles, Career Advice & Habits of Successful People*. In the book, you'll learn from some of the greatest thought leaders of different industries on what it takes to become successful and how to live a great life. I'll also send you a few more of my basketball biographies.

Cheers,

Clayton Geoffreys

Visit me at www.claytongeoffreys.com

Introduction

Everyone knows that basketball is all about developing and mastering a certain set of skills that fit the style of play you prefer. The game is all about knowing the fundamentals and sticking to the development and mastery of those fundamentals until you reach a certain level where you can basically excel in basketball while relying on those skills.

Nevertheless, what is equally true is that a person's physical attributes are just as important in helping a basketball player excel in the NBA. You need to be tall, relative to your playing position, if you want to stand out and become better than all of the other guys playing at your spot. But the one aspect about a player's physical attributes that was often overlooked in the past but is now one of the biggest factors of what makes an NBA superstar is his wingspan.

Throughout the long history of the NBA, there was not a lot of hype surrounding a player's wingspan or length. For example, as dominant of a defensive center as Bill Walton was when he was at UCLA and in the NBA, he never really knew what his exact wingspan was because he never really paid any attention to it back then.[i] But that did not mean that wingspan did not play a role in how a player was able to dominate the NBA game even from the early days of the league.

Many of the league's greatest players were able to climb up to the mountaintop precisely because they had the length that allowed them to excel. At 7'2", Kareem Abdul-Jabbar was said to have incredibly long arms and could easily throw up those skyhooks with ease over the top of any defender. Michael Jordan and Kobe Bryant, two of the greatest shooting guards in the history of the league, played at about 6'6" but sported wingspans of nearly seven feet long. And despite being an undersized center during the "Golden Age" of that position in the NBA during the 1990s, the 6'10" Alonzo Mourning was able to dominate the defensive end and grab rebounds thanks to his wingspan of nearly 7'7".

Today, teams are now paying closer attention to how long a player's arms are because length allows a player to become a better and more versatile defender at a time when teams love to switch defensive assignments.[i] On top of that, players with long arms can easily shoot over the top of any defense and finish strong at the basket over any outstretched arm. That is why the 6'11" Kevin Durant, with his 7'5" wingspan, can basically shoot jumpers over any defender and become a force at the defensive end. Meanwhile, at 6'11" with arms that are nearly 7'4", Giannis Antetokounmpo became the league's most dominant two-way player who can basically dunk over any defender in the paint and protect guards and centers alike with his long arms.

Other players with long arms include the superstar big man Anthony Davis, who has a wingspan of about

7'5" and a height of 6'10". Kawhi Leonard's 7"3 wingspan and height of 6'7" allowed him to win the Defensive Player of the Year not once but twice. And who could ever forget about the 7'1" Rudy Gobert, who came into the league with what was at that time the longest wingspan ever recorded in the NBA Combine at more than 7'9" (later broken by the 7'10" wingspan of Mohamed Bamba)?

All that considered, length is one of the factors that coaches and scouts now look at when they are trying to determine the potential of any player as it has proven to be an advantage on both offense and defense in terms of versatility. And when you talk about a player who may not be the tallest but is certainly long enough to become a very versatile star in the NBA, you have to talk about Brandon Ingram.

Measured at 6'7" without shoes on and more 6'9" when he is wearing his sneakers, Brandon Ingram might not stand out at first due to his skinny frame. Nevertheless, if you look at how long his arms are, you will understand why he was always such a highly-touted prospect ever since he was in high school. Ingram sports arms that are about 7'3" long. As such, it allows him to play a very unique style of play as a small forward who can switch to the guard and the power forward spot on any given day. He has the speed and mobility of a smaller athlete and the height and length that can help him excel against power forwards and even centers. In that sense, it is Ingram's long arms that make him into a matchup nightmare on the court.

Brandon Ingram was always a high-scoring perimeter player when he was at Duke. Even as a freshman, he was already impressing NBA scouts with his ability to play at the perimeter and shoot and finish over any defender using his long arms. He was considered to be a player that could one day develop into an excellent all-around defender because of his ability to cover any position using his combination of length and mobility.

Even so, things started slow for Brandon Ingram when he was drafted by the Los Angeles Lakers in 2016 at the number two spot, despite the fact that the Lakers were already thinking that he had the makings of a future star in the league at a time when Kobe Bryant had just recently retired. They were looking for a future franchise star who could carry the torch and Ingram certainly had the makings of one. But Ingram did indeed falter in his rookie year and could not come out of the gate strong even when the Lakers lacked that reliable offensive punch during their rebuilding period. His shooting from the field was subpar and he was outmuscled by bigger and stronger players.

However, things started to look up for Ingram in the next two seasons as he began to find his shooting touch and develop that reliable mid-range game that allowed him to shoot over defenders much like Kevin Durant. It was in his third season when he truly started looking like a future star when he played together with all-time great superstar LeBron James. With defenses focused on LeBron, Ingram started shooting and scoring better from the floor.

Coming into his fourth season in the league, Brandon Ingram was the centerpiece of a trade that sent him to New Orleans in exchange for superstar big man Anthony Davis. Being sent to a rebuilding Pelicans team looked like a bad situation for Ingram but he made that season his breakout year even when most of the attention and hype surrounding New Orleans were going towards prized rookie Zion Williamson.

Tasked to become the focal point of the New Orleans Pelicans' offense, Brandon Ingram was allowed to take more shots and was shooting more three-pointers than ever before. He used his height to his advantage to get off shots from basically anywhere on the floor and made sure that his length was the defining factor that made his jumpers virtually unguardable.

From averaging 18 points per game in his third year with the Lakers, his numbers spiked to 24 points per game while also rebounding and passing more during his breakout year as a Pelican. He was selected as a first-time All-Star in 2020. Needless to say, Ingram had indeed developed into a star whose potential as an offensive threat had been realized thanks to how he learned to utilize his length to his advantage mainly as a shooter from the field.

Still, at a relatively young age, there is so much more room for Brandon Ingram to grow. He has yet to fully realize his potential or how great an asset his length is, especially at the defensive end of the floor. But while he had indeed transformed into an offensive player that can be compared to Kevin Durant, Ingram's relative youth and long wingspan are going to be vital for his team in the future as he is going to be tasked to do more—and be more—in the coming years of what is surely going to be a bright and long career.

Chapter 1: Childhood and Early Life

Brandon Xavier Ingram was born on September 2, 1997, to parents Donald and Joann Ingram. He was born and raised in Kinston, North Carolina. As we know, North Carolina happens to be a hotspot for basketball talent in the United States and home to some of the best college basketball programs in the country. As such, there was no wondering why Brandon Ingram eventually fell in love with the game of basketball. But what you also must consider is that the sport was always in his blood.

Donald Ingram, Brandon's father, used to be a basketball player but was never able to achieve much success. Nevertheless, he spent a lot of time bouncing around from one semi-pro league to another during his prime as a player. Throughout his travels, he never really got over the hump and was forced to move back to his hometown in Kinston. It was there when he started playing pick-up games with a young teenager named Jerry Stackhouse, a future NBA star who was simply looking for older and bigger players to play with at that time.[ii] Because of the foundation that Donald had with Jerry Stackhouse, the latter would later serve as a sort of mentor for Brandon Ingram, who called the former NBA player "Unc." After his days as a basketball player, Donald spent time working as a police officer and also as a manager of a fitness gym. Nowadays, he works as a full-time welder.

Brandon Ingram grew up having two half-siblings. His older brother is Donovan, whom he shares a father with. Meanwhile, he shares a mother with his older sister Brittany. It was Donovan he was closest to as his older brother—he may have lived in a different house with a different family but he was spending a lot of time during the weekends playing basketball with his younger brother.

Donovan (or "Bo," as he was often called) taught the basics of the sport to Brandon, whom he called a "sponge for basketball" due to how quick he was to absorb all of the necessary fundamentals even when he was still young.[iii] At that time, Brandon was focused more on simply learning how to play the sport rather than anticipating that he would one day develop physical attributes fit for an NBA star.

Growing up, Donovan "Bo" Ingram continued to be one of Brandon's biggest basketball influences as they spent a lot of time together. Even when Brandon was yet to turn into a teenager, Bo encouraged his younger brother to play against bigger and older players, especially those who were teammates with him in many of the different teams he himself played for. Donovan later went on to play for UT-Arlington.[iv]

Meanwhile, at the encouragement of his father Donald, Brandon Ingram was never afraid to go hard against bigger and older players, since he was always told to never have fear in his heart no matter who was in front of him.[iii] This helped the young Brandon Ingram to develop a confident demeanor. Yet as confident as he might have been from an early age, Brandon was always someone who would rather stay cool and quiet. His father describes his personality as laid back and not as vocal or as outgoing as most other types of superstars.[iv]

Nevertheless, that does not mean Brandon lacked the right kind of confidence and competitive spirit in his game. Even when he was young, Ingram channeled all of his frustrations and emotions onto the court and would rather let his game do the talking rather than his mouth.

It was also a good thing that Brandon Ingram was channeling all of his feelings into the game. He grew up in a town that had a particularly high crime rate. But, instead of staying on the streets where he could have met the wrong kind of influences and been drawn towards a different and less wholesome life, he focused more on basketball while looking for the best kind of people to look up to. Those included his dad, his brother, Jerry Stackhouse, and all the older kids he played against.

Due to his early training in basketball, Brandon Ingram grew up knowing the fundamentals of the sport both in terms of how to play it as well as understanding the rules that govern inside the four corners of a court. His father described him as fundamentally sound in terms of skill and knowledge, and that was what allowed him to stay cool and collected on the court regardless of what the referees were calling. The early foundation of playing organized basketball and knowing the rules of the game from an early age helped Brandon realize that getting frustrated at calls and complaining about how the referees were officiating are all useless. Instead, his influences in life taught him that the best way to release his frustrations was to just play harder.[iv]

It was too easy for Brandon Ingram to get frustrated deep inside while he was growing up. He often got criticized by friends and peers alike for being too skinny and for being too quiet or not vocal enough in and out of the court. But while he was indeed skinny, and even though he was always a quiet boy, he always let his game do the talking and it never seemed like he was too skinny when he was a 12-year-old playing against college basketball players. As his father often told him when he was young, Brandon should always go hard with no fear, no matter who he was up against. This type of mentality was what allowed him to keep up with players who were older and bigger than he was.

Meanwhile, Jerry Stackhouse's influence on Brandon Ingram as well as the entire neighborhood of Kinston was felt during the youngster's early years as a basketball player. One of Stackhouse's goals was to try to give children a safe haven where they could spend more time rather than on the street where they could grow up with all the bad influences in life. Basketball was the key to getting those kids off the streets while also providing an avenue for talented children to be able to learn the game.

At that time, Brandon was the one kid who not only looked at basketball in Kinston as a safe haven but also treated it as the stepping stone to a stellar career. Even as a kid, Ingram was already showing the makings of a basketball star. He was always something special and was more than prepared to absorb everything that his youth coaches were telling him. Brandon even went on to play for Jerry Stackhouse's AAU team by the time he reached eighth grade. And he had to travel all the way to Atlanta to play for the former NBA All-Star's team.

Nevertheless, throughout his entire early life, Brandon Ingram stayed in North Carolina due to how much he loved his family and the community where he had learned how to play basketball. He would later enroll at Kinston High School, where he became a productive player and eventually a national sensation after leading the school to four straight state championships.

Chapter 2: High School Career

Brandon Ingram was immediately a part of his high school's basketball varsity team when he was a freshman at Kinston High School in his hometown. However, Ingram started his career as a bench player as he had to play behind the bigger and more established players on the varsity team. After all, he was still yet to grow to his mature height and was still a very skinny boy even though he was already showing promise as a future star. Ingram was about 6'2" in his freshman year and was playing the guard role more than the forward. This was where he developed the point guard skills he would later show off in the NBA.

But as his freshman season continued to unfold, Brandon Ingram's role with his team grew because his coaches realized that he had the kind of rare talent that would one day make him a special player—not only in high school but as a future professional. He played a reserve role for the team but he was receiving touches and getting minutes that not a lot of freshmen were getting. Ingram helped his Kinston High School Vikings beat Cuthbertson in 2012 to win the state championship.

A year later, Brandon continued to grow both in size and in his role with the team, all while continuing to play for Jerry Stackhouse's AAU team during the offseason periods. It was during his sophomore year when Ingram became a full starter for Kinston High School and was becoming one of the team's go-to players on the offensive end.

Brandon played a pivotal role in securing a second consecutive state title for Kinston. While he did not lead the team in scoring, he contributed 12 points to complement the 18 points of their senior star, Denzel Keyes (who later went on to play both basketball and football for the Aggies). In total, Ingram averaged 12.4

points and 3.9 rebounds during his entire sophomore year during the 2012-13 season when he once again helped his team win a state championship.

During the summer prior to the 2013-14 season, Ingram stood out in Jerry Stackhouse's AAU team and went on to impress scouts before his junior year in high school. That was when he truly started to improve his game as he went on to grow both in skill and size. By the time he reached his junior year with the Kinston Vikings, Brandon Ingram had grown to 6'7", which is close to his mature height of nearly 6'9" with shoes on.

Even before his junior year, Brandon Ingram started getting offers from college programs. At that point, the most notable name was the University of North Carolina, which is known as the program where great NBA players and legends such as Michael Jordan and Vince Carter developed.[v] But Ingram wanted to play one more year of AAU basketball the following season because he wanted more coaches to get to see his game and to watch how he improved before making a decision as to where he wanted to go. The consensus was that he was going to become a Tar Heel in North Carolina but the choice was still up to him, as he had already gotten offers from other programs such as Virginia Tech, Louisville, and NC State. Ingram wanted to weigh his options first and see where he would best fit in terms of what the program had to offer and who the players were he would be playing alongside.

Despite the attention he was getting from numerous other programs, the tall and lanky Brandon Ingram was ready to make full use of his length and uncanny abilities to lead his high school team back to a state championship that season. The focus was for him to become the leader he was expected to be and to throw all doubts and fears behind him, or else opposing players and teams might sense his fear and take advantage of it. That was why Ingram was working so

21

hard during practices and was pressuring himself to get better before the games so that he would feel relaxed and at ease when it was time for him to strut his stuff on the basketball court.[v]

True enough, Brandon Ingram improved greatly as a player and as a leader. He went on to lead Kinston High School to its third straight state championship when he dominated the title game against North Rowan with 28 points and 16 rebounds just a year after he scored only 12 points. Overall, the Vikings were 26-4 that season under Ingram's leadership. The 6'7" junior went on to average improved numbers of 19.5 points, 9.1 rebounds, and 2.5 blocks. He was named the Eastern Regional MVP that season due to his amazing numbers and his state-title-winning performance the entire year.

Even though Brandon Ingram was already on the radar of a lot of college programs before he started playing in his junior year, he was an even bigger commodity during the summer of 2014 when he dominated the Norman Parker Showcase as a member of Stackhouse Elite. He was an offensive juggernaut throughout the entire tournament as he was seemingly unstoppable whenever he wanted to score buckets. His performance in the tournament gave him a top-five spot in the entire nation and he was arguably the best high school American at that time. Ingram's ability to drain buckets with ease using his height and length also earned him early comparisons to the superstar NBA player Kevin Durant. The incoming high school senior earned the MVP honors of that tournament.[vi]

Ingram never stopped playing ball during the offseason. He dominated the Adidas Uprising circuit and went on to average 18 points in that tournament. On top of that, he also participated in the NBPA Top 100 Camp, which was reserved for the nation's top 100 players in high school. Ingram also decided to stay in his home state to play for tournaments together with his Kinston High School teammates.

By the time Ingram was about to reach his senior season in high school, he was widely regarded as the second-best player among all high school students in the entire nation and was the best American prep player. The top-ranked high school player was the 6'10" Australian Ben Simmons, who won the NBPA Top 100 Camp MVP Award and was drawing comparisons to both Magic Johnson and LeBron James.

Brandon Ingram led the Kinston Vikings to a 26-4 season in his senior year with the team. His highlight performance that season came when he scored 43 in the opening game of the year. On top of that, he was once again the most outstanding player of the state championship game after he scored 28 points, collected 10 rebounds, and blocked 5 shots to give the Vikings a fourth straight title. Ingram became the first player in state history to win four straight titles. The graduating Kinston superstar averaged 24.3 points and over 10 rebounds a game during his senior year in high school.

At the end of his senior year, Brandon Ingram was ranked as a five-star recruit and was in the top five of scouting experts all over the nation. The consensus was that he was only second behind Ben Simmons overall, but was the best small forward in the entire country.

Indeed, Ingram was a superstar in the making and thus, had a wide variety of choices when it came down to where he could play for college. He was described by a recruiting analyst as the best player in all of North Carolina at that time and far better than anyone else. He would have chosen to go play for the Tar Heels had it not been for an academic scandal that affected his decision.[vii] As such, Ingram decided to play for Duke University, which had just won the national championship barely a month before he made his choice. He would become a Blue Devil under legendary head coach Mike Krzyzewski (or "Coach K") and passed on playing for other notable programs such as North Carolina, Kentucky, and Kansas.[viii]

The story of how Brandon Ingram came to decide to go to Duke started when Coach K himself went to his home in Kinston, North Carolina, together with all the members of his coaching staff. While Ingram loved how Coach K talked about basketball, what he really loved was the fact that the legendary Duke head coach was not worried about the young teenager's physical growth. Brandon Ingram was close to 6'8" at that time but was a skinny boy who barely weighed 200 pounds. Coach K told him that his focus was to try to coach Ingram to grow mentally and adjust to the next level from a psychological standpoint instead of forcing him to grow physically.[ix] That was one of the things that truly endeared Ingram to Coach K and Duke.

Now, Ingram's loyalty to Duke started off when he was still very young. When you live in North Carolina where there are plenty of great programs and schools such as NC State, UNC, and Duke that usually stand out in the national rankings, it can be difficult to choose which team you want to be loyal to. But

Ingram always loved Duke more than the other programs in that area—he even got an authentic Nolan Smith Duke jersey when he was a young boy.

When Coach K visited Ingram, he was reminded about his loyalty to Duke and how he grew up hearing criticisms like "he was too skinny" and that "he was not as vocal and as outspoken as most other basketball players are." To that end, Coach K told the young man the one thing that he needed to hear: Ingram needed to adjust mentally to the next level or there would be no guarantees that he would end up starting in Duke.

While Brandon Ingram thought about what Coach K said and initially realized that it seemed backward, given the fact that most coaches should try to sweet-talk their way into getting top players over to their programs, the kid from Kinston began thinking about it in another light. Ingram realized that what Coach K said was supposed to make him want to earn his spot and to work hard for it instead of thinking that he should be given everything he wanted. That was the deciding factor that made him want to get his own Duke jersey instead of simply wearing the one with the name "Smith" on it.

Chapter 3: College Career

True enough to what Coach K had said and what Brandon Ingram feared, the switch to Duke and the collegiate level was going to be an adjustment. In high school, even though he was skinny, Ingram was always able to take advantage of his height and length to shoot over defenders and to finish over the top of rim protectors. On top of that, his peers and opponents in high school were not overwhelmingly bigger and stronger than this skinny yet tall and long college freshman.

But the college game was different. Defenders were much bigger than he was and he did not have the luxury of pacing himself with his shots because he was yet to earn the opportunity to be the team's top shot-creator. Instead, during his first few games with Duke, Ingram seemed hesitant when taking a shot and was losing confidence whenever he was up against defenders who could simply push him away and bully him. He was afraid of physical contact. On top of that, even if he did indeed take the contact, he missed free throws he never should have missed. One case in point was when he shot 4 out of 11 from the free-throw line while scoring only 8 points against VCU in his fourth game of the season.

Even though Ingram started his first two games scoring 15 and 21 respectively, he ended up struggling in the next five games and averaged only 8 points during that span. In two of those games, Coach K benched him due to how much he was struggling. As such, Coach K called him to his office to talk to him and even asked what happened to the hungry kid he had spoken to nearly two years ago.[ix] Even his coach was aware that Brandon was missing the confidence and fire he had exhibited in high school and was struggling to adjust to the college game.

It took some time, but the adjustment eventually happened naturally for Brandon as he kept on playing games and working on his own skills and mentality to improve as the season went on. Plus, one of the ways he was able to get his confidence back was in classes. At the suggestion of his teammates and friends, he took up a public speaking class as a freshman even though most of his classmates in that course were seniors. He was often put on the spot by his teacher, who gave him no choice but to speak up more and to gain the confidence he needed to speak freely in front of a lot of people—there was no avoidance, it was either go for it and speak up or fail.

For Ingram, the public speaking class was instrumental in helping him regain the necessary confidence he needed. Furthermore, he applied the same go-for-it analogy in basketball. When he was on the court, he had no choice but to take the shot confidently instead of hesitating to attempt the shots he could normally make.[ix]

When Ingram finally got his groove and confidence back, he made a big splash in the collegiate basketball scene. Against Indiana on December 2, 2015, he scored a new college career-high of 24 points. Three days later, he followed up with 23 against Buffalo. Then on December 15th, he had his best individual performance when he finished a win over Georgia Southern with 26 points and 14 rebounds, both of which are career-highs for him in college. He had a similar game against Elon when he had 26 points and 11 rebounds on December 28th.

After scoring only 8 points against Utah State back on November 29th and failing to score in double digits in four of his first seven games, Brandon Ingram went on to go through the entire season scoring in double digits in all but one of the rest of his games. On top of that, when their leading rebounder, Amile Jefferson, went down with an injury after playing nine games, Brandon Ingram stepped up and started rebounding the ball more. This allowed him to collect plenty of double-double performances as a college freshman at Duke.

With the loss of one of their best paint protectors, Brandon Ingram also stepped up big time on the defensive end despite his lack of strength and heft. Using his length to his advantage, he blocked four shots against Wake Forest on January 6, 2016. And a game after that, he broke his career-high in blocks and flirted with a triple-double after going for 16 points, 9 rebounds, and 6 blocks in a win over Virginia Tech.

And Brandon Ingram's confidence and stats were not the only things that were increasing. In fact, Coach K's trust in Ingram was growing at a rapid pace as well. After seeing his prized freshman struggling in his first few games, he quickly noticed that Ingram was indeed adjusting and no longer seemed as nervous as he had been during the early portion of the season. He saw how the young 18-year old was able to shrug off the early-season jitters and grew to become a very confident player who demonstrated that he knew what he was doing on the offensive end. That was why Coach K and the rest of the Duke coaching staff was so eager to give Ingram a lot of freedom on the offense instead of restricting him to a system of designed plays.[x] If you are standing nearly 6'9", have the wingspan of a center, and can create shots off the dribble, you deserve a lot of offensive freedom.

While it was the sophomore guard Grayson Allen who led the Blue Devils in scoring, the widespread belief was that Ingram was Duke's overall best player all season long. Allen showed a craftiness in his offense and was capable of hitting three-pointers at a high rate but he was not someone who could attract the same kind of defensive attention that Ingram was getting throughout the latter portion of the season. As such, it was easy to understand why Coach K was putting a lot of trust in his freshman's game.

Brandon Ingram helped lead Duke to win over NC State in the second round of the ACC Tournament after he scored 22 points against the team that was located barely an hour and a half away from Kinston. However, Duke lost to Notre Dame in the quarterfinals of the tournament as the Blue Devils failed to secure a conference championship heading into the NCAA Tournament.

Nevertheless, the Duke Blue Devils secured an NCAA berth and were a fourth-seeded team. Playing nearly the entire game against UNC Wilmington, Ingram scored 20 points and collected 9 rebounds to help his team advance to the second round. There, they defeated Yale as Ingram was once again spectacular when he went for 40 minutes and finished with 25 points. Duke, however, saw their season end in the Sweet 16 when they lost to Oregon. The loss was not entirely on the broad-yet-lanky shoulders of Brandon Ingram, who finished that game with 24 points.

Ingram finished his freshman year and his lone season at Duke averaging 17.3 points, 6.8 rebounds, 1.1 steals, and 1.4 blocks. He shot 44% from the field and was a sniper from the three-point line after averaging 41% from deep. If he did not have such a slow start to the season, the young Blue Devil might have averaged 20 points a game. The proof of that was when Ingram was even better during the NCAA Tournament where he averaged 23 points.

In what was obviously going to be his lone season in college, Ingram was named the ACC Rookie of the Year and was also an honorable mention in the Associated Press All-American team. With accolades such as those and with the trust and confidence of his all-time great coach, Brandon Ingram was set to declare for the 2016 NBA Draft and was widely considered as one of the two best players in the entire draft class.

After declaring for the draft, Brandon Ingram wrote a letter via *The Players' Tribune* addressed to Duke, which he called home for only a year. He went on to tell a story of how his journey as a Blue Devil began when he wore an oversized Nolan Smith jersey as a young boy and how Coach K personally went to his home to try to recruit him. He went on to narrate how great it was for him being at Duke and how thankful he was for the teammates that he had in that one single season. Brandon Ingram was ready to part ways after fulfilling his dream of becoming a Duke Blue Devil. He was now ready to make a name for himself in the NBA.

Chapter 4: **NBA Career**

Getting Drafted

Ever since he was in high school, Brandon Ingram was regarded as one of the best young players in the country and was well on his way to the NBA as a one-and-done college player. And while he was already a hot commodity when he was dominating the high school scene in North Carolina, he became an even bigger sensation when he was arguably Duke's best player in only his freshman season as a Blue Devil. His success at Duke improved his stock in the 2016 NBA Draft and there was a consensus that he would be taken in the top two.

The 2016 NBA Draft is a class that was already quite talented even before those players got to the big leagues. A total of four players in that class have already made it to the NBA All-Star Game quite early as three of them were first-time All-Stars in 2020. However, even though four players from that class have become All-Stars, you could make the argument that four more players from that draft year have also become good enough to make a claim at an All-Star slot.

Despite the fact that the draft class was as talented as it was, Brandon Ingram was widely regarded as one of the two best players in that class. The other player who could give Ingram a run for his money as the probable top pick was Ben Simmons, a 6'10" point-forward back in LSU. Even though Simmons was not too successful in college, his ability to handle the ball, make plays, and finish at the basket strong at his height reminded people of Magic Johnson and LeBron James. It was not difficult to understand why scouts and coaches were so high on Simmons as they were thinking that he had the potential to become one of the best players of his generation.

Meanwhile, Brandon Ingram himself was still more than capable of making a claim as the top prospect of that year's draft. There were plenty of different upsides to Ingram's abilities and profile as a basketball player. But all of them revolved around his overwhelming potential as a player who could one day develop into one of the most dangerous scorers in the game due to his physical attributes and set of skills.

The one aspect that really jumped out at you the moment you looked at Brandon Ingram was his length. He may be taller than the average small forward as he measures 6'9" with shoes on and is nearly 6'8" without, but it really is the length that will surprise you when it comes to Ingram's physical attributes. While the average person has an arm length that is more or less the same as his height, and while most NBA players have an average wingspan of about four inches longer than their height, Brandon Ingram sports a 7'3" wingspan—at least six inches more than his billed height.

Ingram has the height of a power forward in the modern NBA but the length of a center even though he plays the small forward position. Everything about him starts with his combination of height and length. It allows him to become the supreme offensive threat he always was when he was still in high school and it makes him an asset that could possibly become one of the more versatile defenders in the league.

Speaking of his offense, Ingram's ability to play like a guard despite having the height of a power forward and the length of a center was what was really impressive about his overall skill set. Owing to the fact that he had to play guard when he was in his younger years, as he was only about 6'2" as a high school freshman, Brandon Ingram learned how to handle the ball well enough for his size. That is why, when he was at Duke, 44% of his possessions were coming from pick-and-roll plays where he was the ball-handler, isolations, and dribble hand-offs. That statistic is usually seen in guards rather than small forwards.[xi]

In that regard, Brandon Ingram was often the main ball-handler and go-to guy for Duke because he could handle the ball well and create shots for himself in any kind of situation. On top of that, his height and length allow him to become a matchup nightmare for virtually any other defender. Put a bigger-but-slower player on him and Ingram can use his mobility and dribble skills to create space. And if a smaller-but-quicker defender was keeping up with him, he could simply shoot over the top of the defense.

Speaking of his ability to create shots, Brandon Ingram has already shown a lot of promise as a next-level shot-maker with his impressive ball-handling skills and shooting stroke. In college, he shot 41% from the three-pointer while shooting over five attempts. He was even shooting from the NBA range in some cases. In isolation situations, he relishes creating mid-range shots off the bounce because he is able to keep defenders guessing, whether he would suddenly pull up from the perimeter or go straight to the basket using his long strides. The fact that he is able to hit jumpers against any defender is what allows Ingram to have a wide array of different choices when it comes to scoring. On top of that, he knows how to mix in a few moves such as jab steps and shot fakes whenever he is in isolation situations.

If you look at Ingram's jump shot, it looks fluid and has solid mechanics. Additionally, it seems easy for him to quickly rise up and release his shots over the top of any defender. That was the main reason why scouts and coaches alike were so high on him ever since he was in high school. The resemblance to NBA superstar Kevin Durant was uncanny, especially considering how both of them have the height and length that allows them to create instant mismatches on the floor.

There also was no problem with how Brandon Ingram approached the game whenever he had the ball. While most gifted scorers immediately seek the rim whenever they have the ball, Ingram knows how to create for others as well and he is impressive at using his height and length advantage whenever he is trying to pass the ball to others. He was never the best passer or the most gifted playmaker but he was always more than willing enough to play an unselfish brand of basketball, something that is valued by coaches and fellow teammates alike.

On the defensive end, Brandon Ingram was never a slouch. The usual criticism he received was that he was too skinny to play inside the paint. But when he was playing power forward on the defensive end, especially when Duke lost their starting power forward, Ingram showed a lot of toughness despite his lack of size and strength. He competes hard on the defensive end and he knows how to fully utilize his length to bother and block shots and to get rebounds.

Of course, in a modern-day NBA where defenses love to switch, Ingram's potential as a versatile defender is something to watch out for because he has the length that allows him to play against big men in a small-ball lineup and he has the mobility to keep up with guards whenever he is switched out on them. On top of that, it will be extremely difficult to get shots up on Ingram because he knows how to use his length.

When it comes right down to his potential and his ability to score, there can be no denying that Brandon Ingram had the makings of an NBA star and could very well develop into one of the most versatile two-way players in the league due to his physical attributes. But, then again, there were still glaring reasons as to why he might fall to the number two spot in the draft behind LSU's Ben Simmons.

The biggest issue when it comes to Brandon Ingram is his lack of size. He may be tall, lanky, and long but he was always regarded as very skinny as he weighed only 190 pounds in the days approaching the draft. You can never doubt his toughness and how he seemingly has enough competitive spirit in him to make up for his lack of strength but that would not work at the NBA level where athletes are bigger and stronger than the ones he faced in college.

Ingram's lack of strength could be a big factor on the offensive end because it was evident in college that he struggled to create shots whenever physical defenders tried to disrupt his balance. He does have a good dribble pull-up game but he clearly had difficulties whenever defenders got too physical with him. This would be a problem for Ingram if physical defenders such as the likes of Marcus Smart, Patrick Beverley, or Tony Allen were to defend him in the NBA.

At the half-court set, you could also clearly see how Ingram's slight frame was a significant problem since he only converted 48% of his inside shots whenever defenses were set, as most of his inside conversions came during transition opportunities. Also, teams probably could not rely on Ingram to convert from the post any time soon since he did not appear to have the strength to play the low block, even if he were to play against smaller defenders. He does have the footwork and he can shoot turnaround jumpers over defenders, but Ingram as a post player would be too one-dimensional if he failed to develop physically.[xi]

On the defensive end, it would be interesting to see how Brandon Ingram would keep up against bigger and much more physical offensive small forwards such as LeBron James, Kawhi Leonard, and Paul George. He probably has the mobility and length to keep up with those guys but he may not be strong enough to contain them, especially when they get too physical with him.

Surprisingly, for such a solid and fluid shooter, Brandon Ingram struggled a lot from the free-throw line during his lone season in Duke. He never had that problem in high school but it seemed to have developed only when he got to college. Ingram may be willing enough to get to the basket to take contact due to his fearless nature but he just seemed to struggle a lot from the line for a player who you would expect to shoot in the high 70s or even in the 80s instead of shooting 68% from the stripe.

And while Brandon Ingram does have the makings of a versatile defender in the NBA, his defensive skills were not yet as polished as his offensive abilities. He still needed to work on understanding the fundamentals of defense and to learn how to make sure that he is not always relying on his length to make up for his defensive mistakes. He can be a good defender at the NBA level due to his ability to possibly defend guards and big men alike but the fundamentals still needed a lot of polishing. And a problem related to that is that he can get too sleepy on defense at times due to his quiet and laidback nature.[xi]

That said, the biggest upside to Brandon Ingram other than the fact that he has supreme physical gifts was the fact that he was only 18 years old at draft time. He is a full year younger than Ben Simmons and has a lot of time left to grow physically and mentally. Of course, you also must consider the fact that he was always described as competitive and hardworking. If he could develop his strength and size when NBA trainers and sports nutritionists finally get to work with him, and if he could continue to focus on getting better physically and mentally, he has the potential to become a star in the league.

As such, his upside as a Kevin Durant-like offensive player and the possibility that he could become a versatile two-way player made Brandon Ingram one of the hottest commodities in the entire draft class. His mentor, Jerry Stackhouse, even went on to say that he could have been the top pick of that year's draft depending on what the team drafting first overall needed. But, in many books, he was expected to get picked second behind Ben Simmons.

On the night of the draft, the rebuilding Philadelphia 76ers did indeed take LSU's Ben Simmons with the first pick, believing that he could take the league by storm with his amazing playmaking and ball-handling gifts at 6'10" and because the team needed a playmaker to pair alongside the incoming Joel Embiid. With Simmons taken, the best player left on the board was Brandon Ingram.

When the Los Angeles Lakers, who had also chosen second overall a year ago when they took D'Angelo Russell, were up on the clock, the choice was obvious. They had recently lost the face of the franchise when the late great Kobe Bryant retired at the end of the 2015-16 season. And while Russell had the makings of a possible All-Star player, they still needed to secure their future by adding another key player with true star potential. Thus, they chose Brandon Ingram with the second overall pick of the 2016 NBA Draft.

Grabbing Brandon Ingram with the second pick made sense. He was the most gifted scorer in that draft class and there was no way any team could mess up with that choice as he was unquestionably the best player available. Moreover, Ingram represented the modern-day NBA because of his offensive versatility as a ball-handling forward who could basically play four positions on both offense and defense. And for the Lakers, Ingram was supposedly going to be the start of a new dawn for the rebuilding all-time great franchise.

After Ingram was drafted, Mike Krzyzewski, who was going to be coaching the U.S. Olympic team that year, went on to say that he believed his former Duke player was going to be a star in the NBA even though he only had a season to observe him. Coach K described Ingram as a smart player on and off the floor and someone who was going to be a great fit for any team because of how low-maintenance he was. But, then again, he also said that Ingram was not going to be an instant star but was going to need some time to develop into his own body and adjust to the style of play in the NBA.[xii]

With all that aside, Brandon Ingram was now an NBA player and was drafted by arguably the most popular and successful franchise in the entire world at the time. Nevertheless, as gifted of a player as Ingram was, most analysts agreed with Coach K and thought he was not going to be an instant standout player in the league. After all, he still needed to adjust and develop. But that did not matter at all if you have a kid who is as hardworking and as humble as Brandon Ingram is.

The Slow Rookie Year

The Los Angeles Lakers were a rebuilding and developing team when Brandon Ingram joined. Their squad of core players at that time were all under the age of 25. They were looking to rebuild and restart around assets such as D'Angelo Russell and Julius Randle, but perhaps their best player was the 30-year-old sixth man Lou Williams. Moreover, that team was composed of a lot of ball-handlers such as Russell, Williams, and Jordan Clarkson. That only meant that Ingram was not going to be handling the ball as much as he did when he was at Duke.

Not being able to handle the ball so much was one of the reasons why Duke head coach Mike Krzyzewski thought that his former player was going to have a long development and adjustment process in the NBA. Brandon Ingram, ever since he broke out in his junior year in high school, was used to having the ball in his hands. Even at Duke, he was the primary ball-handler and was given a lot of isolation and pick-and-roll plays.[xii] That would not be the case when he got to the NBA. With so many ball-handlers on the roster, Ingram would not have the luxury of having the ball in his hands a lot of times. Moreover, the Lakers would probably not try to rush things by giving the ball to Ingram in many plays because he still needed to grow mentally and physically as he adjusted. But the good news was, there was no need to rush him, and most people were willing to accept that it might take a year or two for Ingram to acclimate, especially since he was coming into the league at barely 19 years of age and was going to be one of the youngest players in the entire NBA.

Brandon Ingram was slated to play behind starting small forward Luol Deng as one of the first options off the bench on a Los Angeles Lakers team that had plenty of other bench options such as Jordan Clarkson and Lou Williams. So, even if he was to come off the bench, he obviously was not going to be touching the ball all that much as he would be expected to cede possessions over to his ball-handling teammates.

Surprisingly, Ingram actually had a respectable start to the season when he made his NBA debut on October 26, 2016, in a game against the Houston Rockets. In that upset win in favor of the Lakers, the rookie scored 9 points while shooting 4 out of 6 from the field. But, as predicted, exceptional performances were too far in between for the adjusting Brandon Ingram, who struggled to shoot from the field in the early part of his career.

Brandon Ingram's first start that season was on November 23rd against the powerhouse Golden State Warriors featuring Stephen Curry, Klay Thompson, and the newly acquired Kevin Durant, whom he was often compared to. That was the first time Ingram actually matched up against Durant since the 2014 NBA MVP was not available in the first meeting between the Lakers and the Warriors earlier in the season. Los Angeles won their first meeting when Ingram had 12 points and 6 rebounds, his best game at that point in his career.

But in the second meeting, the Warriors pummeled the Lakers and won by 43 even as Ingram finished with a new career high of 16 points while shooting an impressive 50% clip from the floor. In the next game, which was against the Warriors once again, he finished with 8 points and 9 rebounds but shot only 3 out of 18 from the floor. Given his poor shooting percentage in many of the games he played in the early portion of his career, Ingram was obviously still adapting to the physicality of the game, as he never had trouble with his ability to shoot in the past.

However, despite his less-than-stellar performances, Brandon Ingram started getting more minutes when injuries began to ravage the beleaguered Los Angeles Lakers. It did not even matter whether or not Ingram was shooting poorly from the field because the Lakers did not have a lot of capable players they could actually field. But for the young and slender former Duke star, being able to play more minutes and get more touches was a gift that enabled him to fast-track his adjustment to the NBA game. One case in point was when he scored a new career-high of 17 points while making half of his shots in a 33-point loss to the Toronto Raptors on December 2nd.

Another case that clearly highlighted how the Lakers were not only struggling to win games but were also having difficulty staying healthy was when head coach Luke Walton was forced to give Brandon Ingram the starting point guard spot on December 17th against the Cleveland Cavaliers. At about 6'9", Ingram was not supposed to be a point guard but he managed to do well in that game and showed off his ability to handle the ball and make plays for others. He nearly became the youngest player in league history to finish with a triple-double when he ended that loss to the Cavs with 9 points, 10 rebounds, and 9 assists.

Again, despite such performances, Brandon Ingram still had problems from the field and was barely making 40% of his shots. Considering that he was playing for a Lakers team whose fans cannot help but expect the roster's talented players and top draft picks to produce right off the bat, some critics would call Brandon Ingram a bust even though he had just turned 19 a few months back and had not yet had the time or the on-court minutes to fully transition to NBA-style ball. In that case, playing for an all-time great franchise such as the Los Angeles Lakers was both a blessing and a curse for Ingram, as he was beset by external pressures coming from the media and fans alike.

But for all the criticisms that Brandon Ingram was getting at that early part of his career, the eye test would instantly tell you that he was not a bust. Even as a rookie, he was going at his opponents aggressively and was not afraid to make plays for himself and his teammates. He even had the trust and confidence of his head coach, who really believed that he had the makings of a star in the NBA. The aggressiveness and confidence were already there.[xiv] What was lacking was his ability to stay consistent with his shots and to find his place on the offense as he had to make a huge adjustment from college to the NBA. In short, he simply needed to make his shots. His game needed some fine-tuning, but it was not without potential.

It was easy to understand why Brandon Ingram was seen as a bust at that point. Aside from the fact that he was playing for a Lakers organization that was looking for the franchise's next superstar after Kobe Bryant and the fact that he was chosen as the number two pick, he was also being called the next coming of Kevin Durant. And being compared to Durant was frankly a long shot for Ingram, as it would be for any other player no matter how talented. Kevin Durant is a generational talent similar to the likes of LeBron James and Michael Jordan. He is an all-time great. In that sense, calling a player the second coming of an all-time great will only put unfair and unnecessary pressure on his shoulders. In this case, aside from how slender Ingram's shoulders were, he needed time to adjust mentally and to develop physically before he could even try to prove himself.

The adjustment period seemed slow but it was steady. During January of 2017, Ingram actually showed flashes of brilliance but was still largely inconsistent after putting up two zero-point games in a row. But during a certain stretch that month, he averaged nearly 13 points while shooting 47.5% from the field in nine straight games. He also tied his career-high during that run.

And just as expected and predicted by many, Ingram slowly adjusted to the NBA. Early in February, he had a three-game run of scoring in double digits as he averaged 14.3 points while impressively shooting 53% from the field. His production all year long, as well as the lack of other standout rookies that season, helped Ingram's case as well, as he was chosen as a participant in the 2017 Rising Stars Challenge during the All-Star Weekend.

It was after the All-Star break when Brandon Ingram began showing more of what was to come in the future. On February 26, 2017, he finished a loss to the San Antonio Spurs with a new career high of 22 points after making 10 of his 15 shots from the field. Shortly after that, he mounted a personal best of 12 straight games of double-digit scoring. During that run, he averaged 15 points while shooting 52.5% from the field. In one of those games, which was against the Los Angeles Clippers on March 21st, he had 21 points, 5 rebounds, 3 assists, and 2 steals in what was his most impressive performance at that point in his career.

Brandon Ingram actually scored in double digits in all but three of his final 21 games after starting the first 58 games flat. He had 19 double-digit games in his first 58 games but had 18 in his last 21. That was clear proof that Brandon Ingram only needed time to develop and grow into his game. It indeed took time, but the important part was, he was getting better and was indeed adjusting to the new environment he was in.

At the end of what was a pretty uneventful rookie season, Brandon Ingram averaged 9.4 points and 4 rebounds while shooting 40% from the field. He played 79 games and started 40 of them while playing nearly 29 minutes a night his entire rookie year. Ingram might have started his first 58 games averaging 8 points and shooting 36.3% from the field but he ended on a good note after finishing averaging 13.2 points on 47.5% shooting in the final 21 games he played after the All-Star break.

Brandon Ingram was selected to the All-Rookie Second Team but was not even in the Rookie of the Year radar in what was an eventful year for the rookies of the 2016 NBA Draft class. The best rookie that season was the 2014 draft pick Joel Embiid, who did not even win the Rookie of the Year award due to the fact that he did not play a lot of games. It was the surprising 24-year-old Malcolm Brogdon, the 36th pick of the 2016 NBA Draft, who won the award after playing like a veteran all season long.

As for the Lakers, they were once again well on their way to the draft lottery after a poor season marred with plenty of injuries to their key players. The injuries bit them so hard that Brandon Ingram, the youngest player on the roster, was second on the team in total minutes played all season. Despite that, things were looking bright for the Lakers as Ingram was finally beginning to scratch his full potential.

The Rise

While Brandon Ingram had a forgettable rookie year where critics and non-believers were calling him a bust due to his inability to stay consistent at the NBA level, those who observed him closely, especially during the latter part of the regular season, were aware of how much potential this young man had as he entered his second year.

During the offseason, Ingram knew for a fact that the biggest weakness he had in his game was his lack of strength. He was always a skinny boy growing up and he never really was able to bulk up and build an NBA-type body, no matter how much he trained and ate during his younger years. But now that he had the help of NBA-level trainers, especially in a franchise such as the Lakers and a city such as Los Angeles, Brandon Ingram was able to train his body in the best way possible.

Unlike what most people thought, Ingram was told by his trainers that he did not necessarily need to bulk up, especially if his body just was not genetically inclined to gain a lot of weight. Instead, what the young Brandon Ingram needed to do was focus more on strength and explosiveness despite staying close to the weight he had maintained ever since he was a senior in high school. The former Blue Devil's training focused more on performing weight-training workouts that built up his strength rather than his muscle mass. His goal was to build enough power and explosiveness to take contact both on offense and defense.[xv]

On top of that, Ingram also changed his diet and focused more on getting enough food and nutrition into his body in smaller increments rather than in a few big meals. His diet focused more on carbs and protein so that he could gain muscle weight and have enough energy to keep on working hard on his game. Ingram said that he tends to eat a lot during the summer because that is when he is trying to build his body up in preparation for the upcoming season.[xvi]

Meanwhile, as Ingram continued to work on his game during the offseason, the Los Angeles Lakers also decided to incorporate some major changes of their own. After securing the number two pick of the NBA draft for a third straight season, the Lakers took the talented passing point guard Lonzo Ball out of UCLA. To free up the point guard spot, they traded D'Angelo Russell over to the Brooklyn Nets. And one of their more surprising draft choices during that year was a late first-round pick out of Utah named Kyle Kuzma, who came into the league more offensively polished than what he was given credit for. All the changes allowed Brandon Ingram to slide into the starting lineup as the Lakers' new starting small forward.

After scoring only 12 points in his 2017-18 season debut, Brandon Ingram strutted his newfound improvements on the offensive end and poured in a new career high of 25 points on 9 out of 14 shooting from the field on October 20, 2017, against the Phoenix Suns. And that was not a fluke. Five days later, he had his first career double-double when he finished a win over the Washington Wizards with 19 points and 10 rebounds. On November 3rd, he had another double-double when he had 18 points and 10 rebounds against the Brooklyn Nets. Then, on November 15th, he had his best game at that point in his career when he finished with new career-highs on both points and rebounds after going for 26 points and 11 rebounds against the Philadelphia 76ers in his first meeting in the NBA with Ben Simmons.

Ingram was not done showing how much he had improved in just the span of a single season. On November 29th, he matched up with Kevin Durant in that loss to the Golden State Warriors and even managed to outplay the man he was so often compared to. Durant finished with 29 points but Brandon Ingram had a stellar outing with a new career-high 32 points together with 5 rebounds, 3 steals, and 2 blocks. Up to that point of the season, Ingram was averaging 16 points and was shooting well over the mark he had a year ago.

But while Brandon Ingram may have been playing well in his second year in the league and at 20 years of age, the young Los Angeles Lakers were still struggling to win games and even had a nine-game losing streak during the end of December up to the early part of January 2018. On top of that, the injury bug once again bit the Lakers as they started to miss some key players and some point guards who were tasked to help provide stability from a struggling backcourt.

Brandon Ingram, who played a few games as the starting shooting guard position during the early part of the season, had already gotten used to playing in the backcourt as a ball-handler. But when Lonzo Ball went down with an injury, and with no other point guard capable enough to make plays for the team, Ingram started playing point guard more and was even the starting point guard in a few games from January to March.

With Ingram playing the point guard position, the Los Angeles Lakers started winning more games and only lost seven games in the 21 games following that nine-game losing streak they had earlier in the season. Ingram looked comfortable handling the ball and making plays for his teammates during that run. He went on to average 16.5 points and 4.9 assists in that 21-game stretch as a guard for the Lakers. At one point, he almost put up a triple-double after going for 16 points, 8 rebounds, and 10 assists in a win over the Brooklyn Nets on February 2, 2018.

Unfortunately for Ingram, however, he missed 12 straight games during the month of March due to a groin injury. Without him, the Los Angeles Lakers stumbled back into obscurity after what was an impressive 21-game stretch for them. Ingram did indeed return on March 28th to help win a game against the Dallas Mavericks as he poured in 13 points. But he was quickly shelved once again after the next game due to a neck muscle contusion that placed him in the NBA's concussion protocol. As such, he was forced to miss the final seven games of the regular season with Los Angeles struggling in the middle of the pack as the 11th team in the Western Conference.

Brandon Ingram ended his second year in the league playing only 59 games but averaging numbers a lot better than what he had in his rookie year. He was a much-improved player with averages of 16.1 points, 5.3 rebounds, and 3.9 assists while he was shooting 47% from the floor, an impressive number for a perimeter wing player. In that sense, Ingram had silenced his critics and was showing signs that he would eventually live up to his ranking as the second overall pick of the 2016 NBA Draft.

As impressive as the jump in his numbers were, you had to look at Ingram using the eye test to see how much he had truly improved in his second year in the league. As a rookie, he struggled to get to the paint and even to the line due to his lack of strength. He could not work his way against his perimeter defenders when they got physical with him because of how slender and weak he was. But the added strength and muscle mass that he had worked hard to develop during the offseason helped Ingram gain the confidence he needed to get to the basket more using his dribble moves, long strides, and incredible mobility at 6'9". There were games where he could now shrug defenders off when he was going to the basket for an easy finish.[xvii]

But if you want to look deep into the numbers and quantify how improved Ingram was during that season, the metric that really stood out was the fact that he had a significantly higher shooting-foul percentage compared to the last season. Shooting-foul percentage measures how often a player gets fouled when going for a shot. Ingram had a shooting-foul percentage of 15.2 during the 2017-18 season, which was a notable increase from the 12.6 he had in his rookie year. That number placed him within the 97th percentile of the league in terms of shooting-foul percentage. In fact, to put that in perspective, he had a higher shooting-foul percentage than LeBron James, Anthony Davis, and Russell Westbrook, all three of whom were NBA superstars.[xvii] That meant that Ingram was more aggressive going to the basket and seeking contact—it was evident that he had gained a lot of toughness and strength during the previous offseason.

And another notable improvement in Brandon Ingram was the fact that he was willing to finish more at the rim instead of settling for jumpers. At Duke, he was widely considered a perimeter-scoring threat due to his jump shot and ability to create space off the bounce. Meanwhile, he was a struggling finisher inside the paint during half-court sets. But, in the second year in the NBA, he shot 45% of his attempts in the paint. And when he was not going for layups and dunks near the basket, he was stopping closer to the basket to get clean mid- and close-range jumpers.

But, then again, there were still some areas in Brandon Ingram's game that needed work, as he was still learning how to improve his shot-making decisions and on how to make the most out of every possession he got. The most glaring weakness of his game as a second-year player in the NBA was his lack of three-point shooting attempts. This came as a bit of a surprise because he was a willing shooter back in college and his three-point shot was one of the weapons he was expected to have in the NBA. In fact, he was a 40% shooter from deep in college and was never hesitant to take those long shots.

So what had happened to his three-pointer? In his second year in the league, Ingram may have shot 39% from the three-point line but he barely attempted any shot from that area as he averaged only 1.8 shot attempts per game. The biggest explanation as to why he was shooting fewer three-pointers was his burgeoning love for the long mid-range shot, which accounted for 26% of his total shot attempts that season. As such, there were plenty of moments where Ingram would rather go for a long and difficult mid-range shot off the dribble than to shoot it from the three-point line.

A lot of the instances where Ingram was noticeably shy about taking three-pointers came when he played point guard in place of the injured Lonzo Ball. When he had the ball in his hands and was creating shots for his teammates off pick-and-roll situations, he was seemingly more concerned about making plays for others by trying to get closer to the basket instead of taking what was available, such as attempting a three-point shot whenever he had enough space for it. This made him somewhat predictable towards the end of the season as his shot varieties could be broken down to layups at the basket and mid-range jumpers off the bounce.

What does that mean for Brandon Ingram heading into the future? Well, it was good news that he was able to get to the basket more in his second year and was finishing well at the rim. However, if he wanted to continue to rise and become a better player, he needed to diversify his offensive repertoire and add more weapons to it instead of simply relying on a few good moves that could be easily taken away from him by the defense.

A player he could take his cue from is none other than Kevin Durant. While Durant is primarily a jump shooter, he is often regarded as the most gifted scorer in the history of the NBA due to how he has a complete arsenal of moves that complement his unguardable height and length. He could create shots off the bounce and is always seemingly balanced when going for jumpers from the mid-range but he could also get to the basket at will using his slick dribble moves. And while Durant is often described as a perimeter player who shoots a lot of jumpers, his offense is diverse enough that you would not know what he would do next. He can take a three-point shot in your face, stop at a dime off the dribble to drain a mid-range shot, post you up and hit a turnaround, and even drive past by you for a dunk. That is a perfect example of a diverse offensive player who has a complete offensive arsenal.

That being said, Brandon Ingram is not Kevin Durant and it is unfair to compare him to an all-time great, especially at such an early point of the former Blue Devil's career. Ingram clearly has his own identity and uniqueness as a player. Nevertheless, he has certain qualities that repeatedly invite the comparison to Durant, which is why Durant's success serves as such a tantalizing example of what Ingram might aspire to be. Thus, it was important for him to continue to diversify his offensive game to become a tougher player to guard. The next step for him was to continue to evolve and add more weapons to his arsenal so that it would be nearly impossible for any defense to take him away from the game.

LeBron Era, Final Season in LA

One of the most momentous events in the NBA happened during the free agency period of 2018. LeBron James, the best player of his era and largely considered the greatest player in the NBA at that time, opted out of his final year with the Cleveland Cavaliers to become an unrestricted free agent. Subsequently, he decided that he was going to Los Angeles to become a Laker due to a combination of wanting to raise a family in a better and more competitive environment and the simple truth that he wanted to continue the winning decision in the most storied franchise in the league.

With LeBron James in the mix, the Los Angeles Lakers looked like instant playoff contenders and were seemingly on the cusp of what was going to be one of their more successful seasons in recent years after spending their post-2010 championship era in mediocrity. The coming of LeBron James also signaled the young Lakers pieces to adjust to their new teammate, a 34-year-old man who was already in the NBA for more than a decade and a half and was looking to play for championships instead of waiting on the Lakers' talented youngsters to develop.

But one of the more glaring questions with James' arrival was how Brandon Ingram would fit into the mix. Throughout his entire career, ever since he broke out in his later years in high school, he was always a forward who slid between the three and the four from time to time, depending on what was asked of him to do. And, in the NBA, while he did spend some time at the point and shooting guard spots, he was still primarily a small forward.

Meanwhile, LeBron James was still one of the greatest small forwards in the league and was going to own that starting spot in any team played for. The Lakers also had a talented, scoring power forward in Kyle Kuzma, who was expected to build off what was a successful rookie year as an impressively polished scorer. That all meant that Brandon Ingram had to adjust and was going to start at the shooting guard spot for the Los Angeles Lakers.

While Brandon Ingram looked as productive as he was a year ago, there were instances wherein he seemed like he struggled to play alongside LeBron and was more of a subpar player during the first few weeks of the 2018-19 season, even though he was expected to be able to do more now that opposing defenses were looking to guard James more.

Ingram's early part of the season was marred with less-than-ideal events such as when he was suspended for four games due to an on-the-court altercation in the Lakers' second game of the season, which was against the Houston Rockets. He also missed seven straight games in December due to an ankle injury. Brandon Ingram only scored 20 or more points twice in his first 20 games and was only averaging 15 points per game.

But things started looking up for Brandon Ingram again after adjusting to his new role as a shooting guard. In fact, he loved playing shooting guard because he was able to use his length to his advantage over shorter players on both ends of the floor, basically bothering shots with his long arms and shooting over defenders who were too short to contest his jumpers.

However, there were still problems regarding his role as the starting shooting guard. There was no problem with his ability to defend smaller players because of his length. The problem came on the offensive end due to how he was seemingly doing too much to try to take advantage of his height and length when going up against shorter shooting guards. More and more, he was seen trying to get up contested mid-range shots.[xviii] And while he can indeed hit mid-range jumpers off the dribble and over shorter defenders, contested mid-range shots are hardly the hallmark of what makes an efficient scorer in the modern NBA. Moreover, shooting more pull-up jumpers from the mid-range area also meant that he was not fully utilizing the spacing options that LeBron James was giving the team. In short, he still needed to diversify his shot selection and to take more three-pointers.

The Los Angeles Lakers were looking like playoff contenders in the early part of the season and were on pace to make a return trip back to the postseason. However, a groin injury that kept LeBron James out of the lineup for 17 straight games ultimately led to a series of struggles for the Lakers. The injury to James also pushed Ingram back to the small forward spot.

But LeBron James' injury was not the only problem that Brandon Ingram and the rest of the Lakers had to contend with. During the entire season, the Lakers' young core was the subject of trade speculations. The word was, the Lakers felt like they needed another superstar to pair up with LeBron to fast-track their title contention. Anthony Davis, the superstar big man of the New Orleans Hornets, was making it public that he wanted out of his team and that his preferred destination was LA. Pairing LeBron with Davis would have instantly given the Lakers one of the most feared duos in the entire league.

However, the Pelicans were asking too much for Anthony Davis. The offer that they wanted the LA Lakers to tender to them involved Brandon Ingram together with Lonzo Ball, Kyle Kuzma, and other assets. The negotiations between the Lakers and the

Pelicans went back and forth to the point that Ingram often heard his name in the trade rumors. It eventually fell apart when the Lakers ultimately backed down because New Orleans was asking too much for one player.[xix]

Without James, and with his name being bandied about as the subject of trade rumors all season long, Ingram had to perform much better as both a scorer and a facilitator. On December 30, 2018, he flirted with a triple-double when he finished a win over the Sacramento Kings with 21 points, 7 rebounds, and 9 assists. On January 7, 2019, he had his best game at that point of the season after finishing a win over the Dallas Mavericks with a new season-high of 29 points together with 6 assists. And on January 17th, he had a new career high in assists after finishing with 11 dimes in a win over the Oklahoma City Thunder.

As LeBron James was still nursing his injury, Brandon Ingram also had to score more for the Lakers. On

January 29th, he finished a loss to the Philadelphia 76ers with a new career high in points after hitting 16 of his 20 shots for a total of 36 points. Overall, in the 17 straight games that James missed, Ingram averaged 19.2 points, 6.1 rebounds, and 4.1 assists while shooting well over 50% from the field.

And even as James finally returned to the roster, Brandon Ingram's newfound confidence mixed well with the return of the Lakers' superstar. He finally learned how to play alongside the best player in the game while also gaining the confidence and spunk that he had when he was arguably the Lakers' best player a year ago. Since January 19th, Ingram went on a 17-game streak of double-digit scoring that saw him averaging 22.5 points on a 56% shooting clip. Aside from the 36-point game he had in that run, he also scored 32 in a loss to the Memphis Grizzlies on February 25th and 31 points against the Milwaukee Bucks on March 1st. Ingram also went for 27 points and 13 rebounds against the Houston Rockets in a win on February 21st.

After scoring 25 points in a loss to the Phoenix Suns on March 2nd, Brandon Ingram played his final game with the Lakers not only that season but in his career as well. It was discovered on March 9th that he was suffering from a deep vein thrombosis in his arm. This diagnosis effectively ended his 2018-19 run as it was decided that he would miss the rest of the season with the Lakers finishing in 10th place in the West.

In what was another adjustment season for Brandon Ingram, the lanky 21-year-old finished with averages of 18.3 points, 5.1 rebounds, and 3 assists while improving his shooting numbers to 49.7% from the field. He was impressive during the time when LeBron James missed 17 straight games but was even better later when the King returned to the lineup and he learned how to play well with his superstar teammate.

As seen from Ingram's stats that season, it was clear that he had improved once again, even though he was no longer one of the top offensive options for the team with the arrival of LeBron James. What was obvious was the fact that he was now stronger and more explosive than he was in his first two seasons in the NBA thanks to his dedication to building his body up for strength, spending time in the weight room, and improving his diet. His stronger body has allowed him to get to the basket easier. There were even times when Ingram showed off his improved explosiveness by actually dunking on centers and other bigger defenders.

On top of all that, Brandon Ingram had also learned how to better user his length when taking jumpers. He always had fluid mechanics in his jump shot but Ingram did not have a high release back when he was in his earlier years as a player. But, during the 2018-19 season, he began showing off an improved release and adopted a higher release point that is similar to Dirk Nowitzki's shot.[xx] This allowed him to more effectively pull up from mid-range and hit post-up turnaround jumpers over smaller defenders without fearing the chances of getting blocked.

Meanwhile, you could also clearly see how he had improved as a ball-handler and playmaker. Coming into the NBA, Brandon Ingram had always had handles that were similar to that of a guard's due to how he was forced to play the guard spot when he was still a 6'2" high school freshman. But while he already had a respectable ball-handling ability as a small forward, he went on to improve this aspect of his game and was now able to fully realize his profile as a ball-dominant slashing forward who was capable enough to blow by two lines of defenders on his way to the basket.

However, what was still obvious was that Brandon Ingram was still shying away from taking three-point shots and was not able to fully utilize LeBron's presence on the roster. Having LeBron James on the team meant that the Lakers needed to provide a lot of spacing and shooting to take advantage of his ability to attract defenders, break down defenses, and make passes in traffic. But Ingram was more likely to create his own shots in the half-court than to have someone passing it over to him out in the perimeter where he could have gotten up jumpers. And the numbers were clear on that because he was only shooting 1.8 attempts from the three-point line in his third year in the league and was more likely to make dribble pull-ups from the mid-range. His free-throw shooting was also an issue considering that he once again shot below 70%, even after spending three years in the league as a forward who excels at shooting perimeter jumpers.

Despite how Ingram's shot varieties were still fairly limited, he showed a lot of improvement in his ability to finish in the paint and in creating shots from the mid-range using his ball-handling and length. This was good news to the Los Angeles Lakers not because of how having an improved Ingram helped improve their chances the next season but because his trade stock was improving. The goal was still to acquire Anthony Davis in the offseason, and Brandon Ingram was the center of that trade deal. He had played his final year in LA.

The Trade to New Orleans, Becoming an All-Star

During an eventful 2019 offseason that saw a lot of different star players changing allegiances in a span of a few weeks, one other rising star was forced to play for a different team. The Los Angeles Lakers finally got the superstar they wanted when the New Orleans Pelicans were willing to part ways with Anthony Davis after drafting the talented and physically gifted dominant Duke big man Zion Williamson with the first pick of the 2019 NBA Draft.

In turn, the Lakers offered another Duke Blue Devil to complement Williamson in NOLA. The trade that sent Davis to LA centered around Brandon Ingram as

Lonzo Ball, Josh Hart, and other draft rights and picks were traded over to the Pelicans. While the Lakers had the player they needed to play alongside LeBron James and create the most dominant duo in the league, the Pelicans were able to jumpstart their new era and the rebuilding process with a new player. And it was not just Zion Williamson.

The focus of the Pelicans' new era was indeed on Zion Williamson because the world has never seen anyone quite like this 19-year old kid. He was coming into the NBA standing nearly 6'7" but weighing close to 300 pounds. Despite his large frame, he had a remarkable combination of strength, power, explosiveness, and athleticism. It was easy to understand why people were so high on Williamson.

Nevertheless, what the Pelicans did not expect out of Ingram was how hard he worked on his game during the offseason to surprise the world and come out as possibly their best player during the 2019-20 offseason.

Always the quiet young man who did not like having the attention on him, he thrived behind the scenes as the entire world was looking at Zion Williamson. And all the things he worked on were the questionable aspects of his game. Ingram embraced his new team and was striving to become the very best he could be, and in a new environment where he could truly flourish.

Coming into the new season as one of the young pieces the Pelicans could expect to lean on, Brandon Ingram's fit was still in question due to his lack of range. The league was in the middle of a three-point revolution that saw teams relying more on the three-pointer and on pace and space. As such, teams are expected to shoot more perimeter jumpers in a fast-paced game where there is so much freedom of movement and spacing to take advantage of. But with Ingram playing the role of a slasher and mid-range shooter in his first three seasons in the NBA and as other pieces such as Lonzo Ball, Jrue Holiday, and

Zion Williamson were expected to have their own challenges from the three-point line, it was up to the former Laker to create that spacing for New Orleans.[xxi] Meanwhile, repetition was also a key for him when he was expected to get more foul shots as one of the more reliable shot-creators on the roster.

Adding more strength was also a must for Ingram that season. Pelicans head coach Alvin Gentry was a man who loved playing a fast-paced style that favored smaller and more athletic players. As such, Ingram was also expected to play more of the power forward spot, especially with Zion Williamson's surprising and unfortunate injury prior to the 2019-20 regular season. And when Zion did indeed come back, having a small-ball lineup with Williamson at the five and Ingram at the four would be a matchup nightmare for any team in the league due to their speed and mobility. That all meant that Ingram needed to ramp up his work ethic during the offseason to prepare for what was going to be his best year as a professional.

True enough, Brandon Ingram did indeed improve as he took the opportunity he was given to take over when the New Orleans Pelicans were missing the one player who could create shots on his own. Scoring 22 and 25 points respectively in his first two games, Ingram exploded in a loss to the Houston Rockets on October 26, 2019, for 35 points, 15 rebounds, and 5 assists while primarily playing power forward in the absence of Zion Williamson.

But Ingram went on to eclipse his career high in points in a loss to the Brooklyn Nets on November 4th when he hit 17 of his 24 shots to score a total of 40 points. Brandon Ingram actually scored 20 or more points in all but two of his first 20 games that season. He was also averaging 25 points per game during that early part of the season. Unfortunately, his performances could not translate into wins when the Pelicans were only 6-14 early on.

Despite that, Brandon Ingram continued his string of great performances by nearly going for a triple-double on January 8, 2020, in a win over the Chicago Bulls. He finished that outing with 29 points, 8 rebounds, and 11 assists as he was molding himself into a complete offensive package that could score from all areas on the court and make plays for others as well.

Brandon Ingram had another highlight performance when he eclipsed his career-high mark on January 16th. That game was a testament to his fearlessness against big men in the paint and how he did not have it in him to shy away from contact when he repeatedly attacked the basket and the two-time reigning Defensive Player of the Year, Rudy Gobert. Ingram dominated a defensive-minded Utah Jazz team on his way to making 15 of his 25 shots and 16 of his 20 free throw attempts to score 49 big points in overtime. He could have won the game in regulation when he hit a jumper with 0.2 seconds left on the clock but a foul on Gobert sent the game to overtime, where Ingram continued to take over.

While the Pelicans were struggling with only Ingram as their capable scoring option, New Orleans got a lifeline when rookie sensation Zion Williamson finally suited up for them after missing the first three months with an injury. Zion made his debut on January 22nd and was nothing short of spectacular in the games he played even though his minutes and production were limited. But, even though Zion barely played 30 minutes a night, his presence made a difference when opposing defenses were no longer keying in on Ingram.

Zion Williamson's addition meant that Brandon Ingram slid back to the small forward position and that he was not getting all of the looks, unlike before the big teenager's debut. However, he continued to stay efficient with whatever shot selection he had. As a result, the New Orleans Pelicans were winning more games than they did during any portion of the season because they now had new weapons to rely on.

When it was time to announce the All-Star reserves, Brandon Ingram was one of the many players selected to their first All-Star Game appearance in what was a dawning of a new age of young stars in the NBA. The hard work that Ingram put himself through and the patience had all paid off, as he was one of only eight players in the league averaging at least 25 points, 6 rebounds, and 4 assists. More impressively, his numbers were a testament to how he had improved so much as a shooter in all aspects of his game when he was the only player in the league at that time averaging 25 points while shooting at least 45% from the field, 40% from the three-point line, and 85% from the foul stripe.[xxii] If you look at those shooting percentages, they do not look anything like the Brandon Ingram of yesteryear. These were star-caliber numbers.

The New Orleans Pelicans went on an impressive late-season run fueled by Ingram's All-Star appearance and Williamson's return to the lineup. In the 20 games since Zion's return, the Pelicans won 11 and were at a good spot to fight for the Western Conference's eighth seed in the playoffs. However, their contention for that spot had to wait when the NBA games were suspended in the middle of March of 2020 due to the Coronavirus, or COVID-19, outbreak that swept the entire world.

In his first All-Star season, Brandon Ingram averaged 24.3 points, 6.3 rebounds, and 4.3 assists. His numbers all improved across the board as he was the main man for the New Orleans Pelicans and considered to be one of the franchise's cornerstones together with the likes of Zion Williamson and Lonzo Ball. And more impressively, he was shooting efficient numbers of 46.6% from the field, 38.7% from the three-point line, and 85.8% from the free-throw stripe.

While the increased touches and the improved role as the main offensive gun of the Pelicans all contributed to Brandon Ingram's increased numbers, you have to look at the numbers and beyond them to fully appreciate his improvement during the 2019-20 season. First off, as a player who was often described to be too shy in taking three-point shots, Ingram transformed himself into a legitimate outside threat as he was now actually shooting more and more from the three-point line and was averaging 6.3 attempts from that area, while barely going for two three-pointers a game in his first three seasons as a Laker. And this was not a slow and methodical improvement as a three-point shooter. Ingram was always a threat with his jumper but he completely understood how important it was for him to shoot more three-pointers in his fourth season in the league and adjusted accordingly.

Ingram's willingness to take three-pointers added a different dimension to his game as he was finally able to fully transform himself into a complete scorer who could put the ball on the deck and march all the way to the basket using his long strides or take pull-up perimeter jumpers, hit turnaround shots from the post, and kill defenders with his three-point shooting. In that regard, he was now looking more and more like a new-age Kevin Durant due to his offensive repertoire, but he was still his own unique player and poised to carve out his very own legacy in the NBA. Teammate J.J. Redick, a veteran in the league and a former Duke Blue Devil himself, recognized the hard work that his 22-year-old teammate put himself through and said that Brandon Ingram was able to achieve so much in the span of a single year thanks to his dedication to his craft and how he put in the necessary work in the gym during the offseason.[xxiii]

Another impressive aspect that highlighted Ingram's dedication to his craft was when he dramatically upped his free-throw percentage from the 60s to 85.8%, which was the fourth-best shooting clip among all of the players who shot more than five free throws a game. As Redick said, you do not improve your shooting if you did not spend a lot of time in the gym doing all the work and mastering the art of repetition. Brandon Ingram, for all the criticism he got for his slow development in LA, definitely had the talent, skills, and length to become a star, and he was now demonstrating that he had the kind of work ethic needed for an NBA player to become one of the best in the entire league.

When the NBA announced that they would be restarting the season at the end of July in Orlando, Florida, where 22 teams would be vying for a spot at the playoffs, the New Orleans Pelicans managed to earn a spot thanks to how they were able to play well near the end of the season before the suspension. With the Pelicans having a chance to make the playoffs in their rebuilding stage, Brandon Ingram's production will be critically important, especially when he is still yet to play his first postseason in the NBA.

Chapter 5: Personal Life

Brandon Ingram was born and raised in Kinston, North Carolina, where he spent his entire life until he moved to Duke for college. Nevertheless, when he went to Duke, Ingram still remained in North Carolina as he hardly left his home state, which is known for producing top basketball talent thanks to how competitive the college basketball scene in that state is—they have programs such as UNC, NC State, and Duke. It was only when he moved to LA as an 18-year-old when he was drafted by the Lakers that he completely moved out of North Carolina.

As a product of Kinston, Brandon Ingram has known former NBA All-Star Jerry Stackhouse since his childhood years. Stackhouse is a good friend of the Ingram household since Brandon's father Donald knew him when they were younger. The latter went home to Kinston following a short semi-pro basketball career and met the rising young star who was looking for older and experienced players to play with. Since then, Stackhouse has remained close with the Ingram family and he is even addressed by Brandon as "Unc." Brandon Ingram played for Jerry Stackhouse's AAU team in Atlanta during the summers of his younger years where he had the chance to play with other talented players outside of North Carolina.

Ingram has two older half-siblings. He shares a mother with Brittany and a father with Donovan. As to Donovan, who is nicknamed "Bo," Brandon has always been close with his older brother as it was Bo who helped him hone his basketball talents when they were both young. Bo would go to Brandon's house during the weekends to teach his younger brother how to play the game. It was also the older brother who encouraged the younger sibling to play against older players who were already in high school and college. Bo Ingram was a talented player himself who would later play college basketball at South Plains and Texas-Arlington after starring in Kinston High School.

On and off the court, Brandon Ingram is often considered a soft-spoken young man who likes to stay quiet. He often enjoys time on his own and rarely shows his emotions. But, as his father would say, he has a competitive fire that he does not entirely show through his emotions but can be reflected in how he approaches the game with steadfast dedication. Being the quiet young man that he is, Brandon Ingram expresses his emotions through art as he was known in his younger years to draw cartoonish figures of notable NBA players. He even took up drawing when he was at Duke.

Speaking of Duke, one of Ingram's favorite classes when he was a Blue Devil was a public speaking class wherein his teacher would often put him on the spot. While he is not the most outspoken player, he loved the class because he learned how to speak up more in front of other people and he realized that being too hesitant would not help him in basketball or life in general.

Chapter 6: Legacy and Future

When you look at Brandon Ingram, you instantly notice his physical features. Despite his thin frame, he stands at more 6'7" barefooted and more than 6'9" with his shoes on and has arms that go on for days with his incredible 7'3" wingspan. On top of that, he has long legs that have helped him gallop his way to the basket with so much ease. In that sense, he is a perfect basketball player because he is tall, long, and very mobile despite having the height of a power forward and the length of a center.

A lot of the best NBA players in the history of the sport are similarly built. You look at someone like Bill Russell back in the 1960s; he may not have been a seven-foot beast but he was able to hold his own in the paint and become the greatest defender in league history due to his large wingspan. Meanwhile, Kareem Abdul-Jabbar in the 70s and 80s made a living out of hitting the skyhook using his long arms. Even Michael

Jordan and Kobe Bryant, the two greatest shooting guards in history, had long arms that helped them dominate both ends of the floor.

Even in recent years, you have to look at the likes of Kevin Durant, Kawhi Leonard, and Giannis Antetokounmpo, who are three of the best forwards in the league today. Durant and Antetokounmpo both stand nearly seven feet tall but have some of the longest arms in the league, helping them finish over the top of defenders and also play spectacular defense on the other end. Meanwhile, Leonard's long wingspan also allows him to be one of the best perimeter defenders in the league.

In that sense, there are a lot of advantages a player can have when his arms are far longer than average. It allows him to shoot over defenders, finish inside the paint on top of defenses, and bother opposing offenses by contesting shots or going for steals at the passing lanes. And while a long wingspan may be one of the best attributes a player can have, it has only been in recent years that the NBA actually began monitoring wingspan and how it helps players succeed and stand out in the league.

With all that said, Brandon Ingram's physical gifts are what have allowed him to become the star that he is today. You can say a lot about his skills and his work ethic, but Ingram's long arms have always been his key asset. He has the mobility of a guard but is great at using his height and length on offense so that he can basically shoot over defenders uncontested, finish in the lane with ease, and become a defensive gem when he is locked in.

Because of Brandon Ingram's length, skill set, and overall mobility at the forward position, he is often compared to Kevin Durant as he seems to be a legacy player that started when KD himself started showing to the NBA what his height and wingspan could do at the offensive end, especially when you pair it up with the ball-handling of a point guard and the stroke of a shooting guard.

What that ultimately means is that Brandon Ingram's legacy is one of continuation. He epitomizes a new age in the NBA and continues a legacy of versatile players who can do a lot on the floor precisely because they are tall and long but have skills and abilities that are well beyond traditional positions. He is the type of player who has the opportunity to carve out his own legacy and become someone who is not merely a clone but is just as unique as any other star in the history of the game. And the best way for Ingram to do that is for him to take full advantage of his height and length in the best way possible and in whatever manner he deems fit for his own unique playing style.

Another noteworthy advantage that Brandon Ingram has due to his wingspan is his overall versatility at a time when the NBA is now doing away with traditional positions. A lot of teams are now playing a position-less style of basketball that is predicated more on skill and athleticism instead of size and specific abilities relative to a certain position. That is why we are now seeing more and more seven-footer shooting jump shots and small forwards moving up to the center position in some cases.

Brandon Ingram's length and mobility allow him to fit into the mold of what it means to be a position-less basketball player. Traditionally a small forward, he has played four positions in the NBA since the time he arrived at the league, primarily because of how versatile he is with his height and length. He has the ball-handling and passing skill that allows him to play point guard. He can keep up with shooting guards and create shots at that position. And because more and more power forwards are now getting smaller in today's league, it does not even bother Brandon Ingram that he has a slender frame whenever he is moving up to the big man position to stretch the floor and increase the pace for his team.

Unquestionably, Brandon Ingram is the perfect fit for the style of play in the NBA today due to his versatility, as he can basically play four positions and perform well on both offense and defense. He is a great addition to a team that loves a fast-paced style and would prefer to increase the floor spacing. That is why Alvin Gentry of the New Orleans Pelicans was able to use him at the power forward position in only his first year with that team. And the more Ingram adds strength to his frame while improving his defensive skills, you can only imagine what he may do as a versatile position-less player in the future when the NBA moves closer and closer to doing away with the traditional positions in basketball.

At this point in his career, Brandon Ingram has not yet accomplished enough to warrant the same kind of recognition that some of the other stars in the league get. He is not quite there yet and he still has a lot of room left to grow if he wants to truly rise as a superstar. It is only when he has truly reached his full potential that he may be considered one of the greats of his era, no matter what position he plays.

The reality is, Ingram is a relatively young star who is still just scratching the surface of his potential. Plenty of players at his age were nowhere near as good as he is at this point in his career, and Ingram still has room to grow physically and mentally. And, as far as many people are concerned, his unstoppable work ethic is what has allowed him to truly rise to stardom. No one has worked harder or with more dedication than Brandon Ingram. And when you factor in his length, the sky is literally and figuratively the limit for this long, wiry, and remarkably talented young man.

Final Word/About the Author

I was born and raised in Norwalk, Connecticut. Growing up, I could often be found spending many nights watching basketball, soccer, and football matches with my father in the family living room. I love sports and everything that sports can embody. I believe that sports are one of the most genuine forms of competition, heart, and determination. I write my works to learn more about influential athletes in the hopes that from my writing, you the reader can walk away inspired to put in an equal if not greater amount of hard work and perseverance to pursue your goals. If you enjoyed *Brandon Ingram: The Inspiring Story of One of Basketball's Star Forwards,* please leave a review! Also, you can read more of my works on *David Ortiz, Mike Trout, Bryce Harper, Jackie Robinson, Aaron Judge, Odell Beckham Jr., Bill Belichick, Serena Williams, Rafael Nadal, Roger Federer, Novak Djokovic, Richard Sherman, Andrew Luck, Rob Gronkowski, Brett Favre, Calvin Johnson,*

Drew Brees, J.J. Watt, Colin Kaepernick, Aaron Rodgers, Peyton Manning, Tom Brady, Russell Wilson, Odell Beckham Jr., Bill Belichick, Charles Barkley, Trae Young, Gregg Popovich, Pat Riley, John Wooden, Steve Kerr, Brad Stevens, Red Auerbach, Doc Rivers, Erik Spoelstra, Michael Jordan, LeBron James, Kyrie Irving, Klay Thompson, Stephen Curry, Kevin Durant, Russell Westbrook, Anthony Davis, Chris Paul, Blake Griffin, Kobe Bryant, Joakim Noah, Scottie Pippen, Carmelo Anthony, Kevin Love, Grant Hill, Tracy McGrady, Vince Carter, Patrick Ewing, Karl Malone, Tony Parker, Allen Iverson, Hakeem Olajuwon, Reggie Miller, Michael Carter-Williams, John Wall, James Harden, Tim Duncan, Steve Nash, Draymond Green, Kawhi Leonard, Dwyane Wade, Ray Allen, Pau Gasol, Dirk Nowitzki, Jimmy Butler, Paul Pierce, Manu Ginobili, Pete Maravich, Larry Bird, Kyle Lowry, Jason Kidd, David Robinson, LaMarcus Aldridge, Derrick Rose, Paul George, Kevin Garnett, Chris Paul, Marc Gasol, Yao Ming, Al Horford,

Amar'e Stoudemire, DeMar DeRozan, Isaiah Thomas, Kemba Walker, Chris Bosh, Andre Drummond, JJ Redick, DeMarcus Cousins, Wilt Chamberlain, Bradley Beal, Rudy Gobert, Aaron Gordon, Kristaps Porzingis, Nikola Vucevic, Andre Iguodala, Devin Booker, John Stockton, Jeremy Lin, Chris Paul, Pascal Siakam, Jayson Tatum, Gordon Hayward, Nikola Jokic, Bill Russell, Victor Oladipo, Luka Doncic, Ben Simmons, Shaquille O'Neal, Joel Embiid, Donovan Mitchell, Damian Lillard and *Giannis Antetokounmpo* in the Kindle Store. If you love basketball, check out my website at claytongeoffreys.com to join my exclusive list where I let you know about my latest books and give you lots of goodies.

Like what you read? Please leave a review!

I write because I love sharing the stories of influential athletes like Brandon Ingram with fantastic readers like you. My readers inspire me to write more so please do not hesitate to let me know what you thought by leaving a review! If you love books on life, basketball, or productivity, check out my website at claytongeoffreys.com to join my exclusive list where I let you know about my latest books. Aside from being the first to hear about my latest releases, you can also download a free copy of *33 Life Lessons: Success Principles, Career Advice & Habits of Successful People*. See you there!

Clayton

References

[i] McCauley, Janie. "NBA teams paying closer attention to players' wingspan". *Wisconsin State Journal*. 13 April 2018. Web.

[ii] McGee, Ryan. "Brandon Ingram's rise has brought a whole new batch of Duke fans". *ABC News*. 25 March 2016. Web.

[iii] Norlander, Matt. "Duke's Brandon Ingram is a rare case of a quiet, creative superstar". *CBS Sports*. 16 March 2016. Web.

[iv] Gleeson, Scott. "NBA-bound Brandon Ingram cool on the surface, fiery beneath it". *USA Today*. 22 June 2016. Web.

[v] Young, Justin. "Elite programs in to see Brandon Ingram, focus remains on state championship". *Hoops Seen*. 4 September 2013. Web.

[vi] Wilson, Carter. "The first time I saw Brandon Ingram". *Hoop Seen*. 23 June 2016. Web.

[vii] Wertz, Langston Jr. "Elite recruit Brandon Ingram's attention on 4th title, then decision". *Charlotte Observer*. 123 March 2015. Web.

[viii] O'Donnell, Ricky. "5-star wing Brandon Ingram commits to Duke". *SB Nation*. 27 April 2015. Web.

[ix] Ingram, Brandon. "Farewell, Duke". *The Players' Tribune*. 5 April 2016. Web.

[x] Bohlin, Michael. "Coach K has sent Brandon Ingram letters during his rookie season". *CBS Sports*. 20 December 2016. Web.

[xi] *Draft Express*. Web.

[xii] Ramirez, Joey. "Coach K Foresees Ingram Becoming 'Very Special Player'". *NBA.com*. 19 July 2016. Web.

[xiii] Torres, Aaron. "Coach K: here's what Brandon Ingram needs to become an NBA star". *Fox Sports*. 15 November 2016. Web.

[xiv] Oliver, Jason. "Los Angeles Lakers: Ingram looks like a bust, but he isn't". *Hoops Habit*. January 27, 2017. Web.

[xv] Lane, Trevor. "Lakers News: Brandon Ingram Taking His Strength Training To The Next Level". *Lakers Nation*. 9 August 2017. Web.

[xvi] Darby, Luke. "The Real-Life Diet of Brandon Ingram, the NBA's Most Talented Beanpole". *GQ*. 15 January 2018. Web.

[xvii] Regla, Alex. "Brandon Ingram was a completely different player in year two". *SB Nation*. 18 April 2018. Web.

[xviii] Irwin, Anthony. "Brandon Ingram likes starting at shooting guard". *SB Nation*. 1 November 2018. Web.

[xix] Hartwell, Darren. "Anthony Davis likes Lakers' final trade offer for him (on Instagram, anyway)". *NBA Sports*. 5 February 2019. Web.

[xx] Ellentuck, Matt. "Why Brandon Ingram suddenly looks like a star". *SB Nation*. 4 March 2019. Web.

[xxi] Quinn, Sam. "Inside the minor tweaks that could finally turn former No. 2 pick Brandon Ingram into an All-Star". *CBS Sports*. 9 January 2020. Web.

[xxii] "Brandon Ingram named a reserve for 2020 NBA All-Star Game". *NBA.com*. 30 January 2020. Web.

[xxiii] Eichenhofer, Jim. "Work ethic led to Brandon Ingram's vast improvements in 2019-20, first All-Star appearance". *NBA.com*. 14 February 2020. Web.

Printed in Great Britain
by Amazon